A Bucketful of Ideas for Church Drama

12 skits, sketches and
puppet shows
for schools, churches and
family fun

by
Fay Rowland

Visit the author's website at www.fayrowland.co.uk

Typeset in Century Gothic 11pt for high legibility.

ISBN: 9781549710575

Contents

Introduction - very short, I promise

I know you want to get to the main course, so I'll make the starter very small – like tiny thimbles of tomato soup, or microscopic squares of toast with caviar.

You have in your hands A Bucketful of Ideas for Church Drama, in other words, scripts. They are suitable for:

- church services

- holiday clubs

- youth / kids / toddler groups

- school assemblies

- family fun days

- beach missions

- street drama

- Messy Church

The scripts do not require lavish costumes or scenery, and most can be played by people or by puppets, depending on whom you have available. There are some ideas about using puppets and making a simple puppet theatre at the end.

Most of the sketches have a bright and cheery feel, and tell familiar Bible passages with fresh 'oomph!' Others are more quiet and reflective, such as 'A Bad Friday', which could be used as a Good Friday meditation – accessible for children, while thought-provoking for adults.

Many of the dramas in this book were first written for the children's ministry at St Bot's (yes, that really is a church) and have been refined to as near perfection as I can get

1

in the fearsome furnace of the five-year-old's response. Never has there been a more severe critic!

Some sketches have appeared in larval form in The Reflectionary, a weekly blog of resources for active worship. You can follow The Reflectionary on facebook, on twitter @Reflectionary_ (please note the underscore), or sign up to have the golden globs of goodness sent to your inbox weekly by visiting www.reflectionary.org.

If you like this, why not see other publications from the same author? Visit www.fayrowland.co.uk (There are freebies!)

Now, bring on the ideas!

The Scripts

Each chapter has these sections:

- Outline

- Characters

- Costumes and Props

- Staging

- Script

The first section is an outline of the story. Most are based on passages from the Bible, while others explore Christian themes.

Next, there is a list of characters, with guidance on casting. A part marked 'person' can be played by anyone old enough to read fluently, learn lines and act, so teenagers and confident older children would usually be fine.

A part marked 'puppet' can, of course, be played by a person, but not always the other way around because of handling props. But you can decide what will work best in your situation.

The next section has costume suggestions, and a list of props that the script refers to. You can add extra props or costuming if you wish, depending on what you have available.

The section on staging gives brief notes on any chairs, tables or similar that are needed. Again, you can add to the scenery if you have the facilities. This section also gives general placement of main characters and their starting positions.

Feel free to adapt the words to suit your actors and audience. Generally, scripts work best when the actors are saying words they are comfortable with, and moving in a way that feels natural.

In the script itself, there are few stage directions, but where they are needed, you will find them in square brackets, [like this].

Some scripts are interactive, with audience responses in round brackets, (like this). Having some 'plants' in the audience is a good way to encourage a quiet crowd. (Oh No It Isn't!)

Elijah and the Ravens

Outline

My parrot puppets were complaining that they didn't have many opportunities to perform, so I promised I would write a sketch especially for them. Here is the result.

This sketch reveals what was *really* going on at the Cherith Brook with those 'ravens'. (1 Kings 17:1-6)

Characters

- Elijah - person
- Parrot 1 - puppet
- Parrot 2 - puppet

You can substitute any brightly-coloured bird puppets – the less they look like ravens the funnier it will be. If you do not have bird puppets you can have fun making your own gaudy sock puppets with dyed feathers, as garish as you like.

Parrots 1 and 2 can be played by one puppeteer.

Costumes & Props

Elijah needs a telephone, a small suitcase with holiday contents, and a mug.

Parrots 1 and 2 can wear holiday gear such as flower garlands or sun hats, if you have any to fit.

Parrot 2 needs a lunch box.

Staging

The phone needs to 'ring'. This can be done with an actual ring tone played through the PA system, or by the actor simply saying 'ring-ring'. You could add this as an audience participation by having 'ring-ring' on a large card to display at the appropriate times.

The puppet theatre stands at one side of the stage, designated the 'brook' side. If you have blue fabric you can use it to show the water there. You could add buckets and spades to boost the holiday feel.

Elijah starts at the other side of the stage. He can be seated at a desk sorting paperwork. This will allow Elijah to have a script for the first section which contains most of his lines. The second half, by the brook, has fewer lines and can be learned easily.

Script

Elijah and the Ravens

[ring-ring]

Elijah:
[answering phone]
Hello, this is Elijah the prophet – 'No message too big, no message too small' …

Oh, hello God. Good to hear from you again.
How are you doing? …
umm hmmm …
umm hmmm …

That's nice. And your lad, he's well?
umm hmmm …
umm hmmm …

That's good to hear. So what can I do you for today?
umm hmmm …
umm hmmm …

A message you say?
Well, look no further than Elijah the prophet – 'No message too big, no message too small' …
Oh yes. You're right. I already said that. Sorry. So what's your message then?
umm hmmm …
umm hmWHAT?

You want me to say THAT?
To HIM?
You sure? …
Yes, Ok then …
Bye.

[to audience, looking scared]
Well, this is going to be a scary job! The king in my country is nasty-mean-rotten King Ahab. He has been doing lots of bad things.

God wants me to tell nasty-mean-rotten King Ahab that there is not going to be any rain until he stops being bad and starts being good.

That's going to make the king very angry. So now he'll be nasty-mean-rotten-*angry* King Ahab!

Oh dear. I really don't want to be near him when I give the bad news. Perhaps I'll just call him on the telephone instead.

[dials number and waits]

Oh Hello. Is that the royal palace? I'd like to speak to nasty-mean-ro … umm … I mean I'd like to speak to His Majesty King Ahab please.
No, I don't know the extension.
Thanks.

King Ahab? I have a mess …

[to audience]
Oh. It's gone to voice mail. 'Leave a message after the tone'.
Honestly. Propheting ain't what it used to be, you know.

[to phone]
This is a message for King Ahab from God.
You have got to stop doing bad things. God has told you this lots of times before but you have not listened. So now God will stop the rain in all your land so that you know you have to change.
So there!
Lots of love, Elijah xxx

[puts phone down]

[to self]
Actually, there's a problem with that. If there's no rain then there won't be any water, so what am I going to drink? And if there's no water then the plants won't grow, so what am I going to eat?

[ring-ring]

Hello, this is Elijah the prophet – 'No message to big, no mess ...

Oh hello God. Yes, I gave him the message like you said, but there's a problem ...
Oh, you've already thought of that?
umm hmmm ...
umm hmmm ...

Ravens? You mean the big, black, really mean-looking birds? You sure? ...
umm hmmm ...
umm hmmm ...

Yes, Ok then ...
Bye.

[packing suitcase]

Well that is kind. God has already thought about what I'll need to eat and drink. He told me to go on a bit of a holiday, to a place that has water to drink, and he'll send some ravens to bring me food.

[whispering]
I'm not too sure about the ravens. They're big and black and really mean-looking, but I suppose God knows what he's doing.

Anyhow, I'm pleased about the holiday. I want to get away from nasty-mean-rotten King Ahab because he'll be in a nasty-mean-rotten mood when he picks up that message.

- can break action at this point -

[walks across stage to puppet theatre, taking suitcase and mug]

So here I am and, just like God said, here's a little stream. And I've brought a mug with me, so I'll have plenty to drink.

[indicates long distance just walked]
I think I'll have a bit of a rest after my 'long' journey.

[settles down for a nap and looks into sky away from puppet theatre]
I wonder when the food will arrive?
[yawning]
God said something about ravens bringing stuff, but I can't see any ravens round here. Perhaps you could keep a look out for them. They're big and black and really mean-looking.

[falls asleep]

[Parrot 1 and Parrot 2 enter]

Parrot 1:
You know, I think it's a flippin' cheek.

Parrot 2:
Oooh yeees.

Parrot 1:
'Ere we are, on our 'olidays like ...

Parrot 2:
Oooh yeees.

Parrot 1:
... an' God only ups and tells us to get workin'.

Parrot 2:
Oooh yeees.

Parrot 1:
I mean, makin' us get bread an' meat for some bloke –
Elijeewassit.
What does God think we are, waiters?

Parrot 2:
Oooh yeees.

Parrot 1:
Yes?

Parrot 2:
I mean, Oooh Nooo.

Parrot 1:
Anyway, I s'pose we'd better do what The Boss says.
'Ave you got them 'am 'amwiches?

Parrot 2:
Oooh yeees.
[produces lunch box]

Parrot 1:
Oy! You!
Elijeewassit!

Elijah:
[waking suddenly]
Yes? What?
This is Elijah the prophet – 'No message too bi ...

Parrot 1:
Yeah, yeah.
We knows who you are. 'Ere's your lunch.

Parrot 2:
Oooh yeees.

Parrot 1:
We'll be back at tea-time with some more.

Parrot 2:
Oooh yeees

Parrot 1:
An' make sure you don't drop no crumbs!

Parrot 2:
Oooh yeees.
I mean, Oooh Nooo.

Elijah:
[looking closely at parrots]
Do you mind if I ask a question?

Parrot 1:
Well you just gorn an' asked one!

Parrots 1 & 2:
Ha ha ha ha!

Parrot 1:
Na, alright then. What's your question?

Elijah:
God said he would send ravens with food.
Are you ravens?

Parrot 2:
Oooh yeees.

Elijah:
You don't look like ravens.

Parrot 1:
Well you don't look like a prophet, but I ain't saying nuffin'!

Elijah:
But ravens are big and black and really ...
[realising what he is about to say]
... really nice to meet you!

[shakes wings with parrots]

Parrot 1:
Look, we're on our 'olidays, OK?
We don't 'ave to wear the uniform on 'oliday, we can wear what we likes.
This is our casual plumage.

Parrot 2:
Oooh yeees

Elijah:
Casual plumage?
OK, well I guess that explains it.

[looking at lunchbox]
Thanks for the lunch. What's in it?

Parrot 1:
The Boss said bread an' meat, so we bunged some 'am 'amwiches in there, an' a sausage roll, an' we was plannin' on a nice bacon butty for tea.

Parrot 2:
Oooh yeees.

Elijah:
Oh, ummmn, that's really kind, but I'm Jewish, so I'm not actually allowed to eat ham and bacon and things.

Parrot 2:
What? Not even a bacon butty?

Elijah:
Not really.

Parrot 1:
[to Parrot 2]
Well, that's funny 'cos I 'appen to know that The Boss is partial to a bacon butty of a mornin'.

Parrot 2:
Oooh yeees.

Elijah:
I don't suppose you'd have a little roast quail, would you?
Perhaps some char-grilled chicken?
Kipper paté with capers?
Caviar?

[Elijah moves within striking distance of parrots]

Parrot 2:
Oy! Don't push it, mate!

Elijah:
And, if you can manage it, I'd prefer organic ...

Parrot 2:
He pushed it!
Gerrim!

Parrots 1 & 2:
[jumping at Elijah]
ARGHHHHH!

[Elijah shrieks and runs off]

Very Important People

Outline

This drama tells of Jesus welcoming the children. (Matthew 19:14, Mark 10:13-16, Luke 18:16). They want to meet Jesus, but a disciple will only let in Very Important People. Who counts as important in the kingdom of God?

The disciple is played as a security man or 'bouncer', all gruff voice, folded arms and dark glasses.

Characters

- **Jesus** - person
- **Narrator** - person
- **Bouncer** - person
- **Children** - puppet or person
  plus non-speaking puppets or children (who can be from the audience)

You can do this sketch with just two actors, or with three or four.

If you only have two actors, co-opt a man from the audience to play Jesus. (There are very few words, which you can write on a slip of paper hidden in Jesus's Bible.) Then one actor can combine Narrator and Bouncer (see staging below), while the other actor says the Children's lines.

For three people, either co-opt a man for Jesus and have separate actors for Narrator, Bouncer and Children, or double-up Narrator and Bouncer and have an actor each for Jesus and Children.

One actor or puppet speaks the lines for Children, with the rest of the crowd being non-speaking children or puppets. You can draw them from the audience and they simply need to nod and repeat what the actor says, and move when told. An adult speaking the Children's lines should kneel to be child height and speak their lines using a child-like voice.

Costumes & Props

Jesus can have a Bible, partly to be telling a silent story and partly to hold his lines if co-opted from the audience.

Place a note like this this in the Bible:

You are playing Jesus. You only speak once, right at the end.

Start by sitting down, facing away from the action and silently pretend to tell a long and interesting story to a crowd off stage.

You come in just after the children have put on disguises. Here is your cue:

Bouncer:
No. Jesus is too busy.
Listen, he's talking about very important stuff, and it's only for very important people.

Jesus:
[Half turning so that we can hear what he's saying to the invisible crowd]
... and so you must let the little children come to me
and do not hinder them,
for to such belongs the kingdom of heaven.

[looking round and seeing children]

Ah, hello children! I was wondering when you'd get here.
Come along, I've got some wonderful things to tell you about God.

[children go and sit by Jesus as he resumes talking silently to crowd]

Narrator can read from a script on a lectern.

Bouncer can wear shades or hold a clipboard (which can hold the script)

Children (played by people or puppets) can wear their hair in bunches or hold toys. Actual children are fine just as they are.

Children will need disguises, such as grown-up hats, sunglasses, beards etc. These can be in a box ready for use.

Staging

Jesus is seated to one side, facing away from action. He is talking silently to an invisible crowd, and continues to do so until his lines near the end.

If you are using two people for Narrator and Bouncer, the Bouncer blocks the path to Jesus, and the Narrator stands at a lectern on the opposite side.

If you are combining the parts, Narrator/Bouncer stands at a lectern near Jesus to read the Narrator parts and steps aside blocking the way to speak the Bouncer parts.

Children are gathered centre stage. Adults should kneel to mix with the crowd. If you are using puppets, do not have them in a theatre because they have to move to Jesus. The puppeteer can simply hold them at head height and talk to them as if they were all people.

Script

Very Important People

Narr:
One day, Jesus was talking to the people.
He was telling them about God – how much God loves them and wants them to love him too. There were some children nearby, and they wanted to hear about God, just like the grown-ups.

Children:
[to non-speaking children]
Let's go and listen to Jesus, shall we?
[children agree and move towards Jesus]

Narr:
So the children tried to go to Jesus, but the grown-ups would not let them.

[if using one person for Narr and Bouncer, Narr steps away from lectern, blocking path to Jesus]

Bouncer:
Oy, you can't go in there!

Children:
But we've come to see Jesus.

Bouncer:
Nope, Jesus is busy. You'll have to go away.
[taps clipboard, if used]
If your name's not down, you're not coming in!

Children:
Oh, right. Sorry.
[children go away sad]

Narr:
So the children went away sad.
(ahhh)
They were sadder than that.
(Ahhhhh!)

Children:
What shall we do? I really want to listen to Jesus, don't you?
[children agree]

What's that you say? We could try to tiptoe in? That's a good idea!
[children tiptoe towards Jesus behind Bouncer]

Narr:
So the children tried to tiptoe in to see Jesus. They crept around behind some bushes and were nearly there when ...

Bouncer:
Oy! You lot!
Didn't I tell you to go away? Now hop it!

Children:
Oh, right. Sorry.
(ahhh)

Narr:
They were still sad, you know.
(Ahhhhh!)

So they tried another idea – disguises!
[children put on disguises]

They put on hats and sunglasses and scarves and tried to pretend they were grown-ups.

Children:
This is bound to work this time. Don't you think?

[children agree]
We're sure to get to Jesus. What do you think he's saying?

Narr:
So the children boldly walked up to where Jesus was talking.
[children walk up to Bouncer]
Will they get through this time? Let us see ...

Children:
[in deep voice]
Excuse me please, stand aside. We are very important people who have come to see Jesus.

Bouncer:
Really? Very important people?

Children:
Yes, and we're grown-ups too. We're not children in disguise or anything.

Bouncer:
Are you sure? 'Cos I think you're the cheeky young children who keep trying to see Jesus.

Children:
[in normal voice]
Drat! Foiled again!
But we really, really want to see Jesus. Can't we come in pleeeeeeease?

Bouncer:
No. Jesus is too busy.
Listen, he's talking about very important stuff, and it's only for very important people.

Jesus:
[Half turning so that we can hear what he's saying to the invisible crowd]
… and so you must let the little children come to me and do not hinder them,
for to such belongs the kingdom of heaven.

[looking round and seeing children]

Ah, hello children! I was wondering when you'd get here.
Come along, and sit by me. I've got some wonderful things to tell you about God.

[children go and sit by Jesus as he resumes talking silently to crowd]

Bouncer:
[pretending that is what he had meant all along]
Well, yeah. That's what I said. Jesus is talking only to very important people.

Snuffles and the Big Bad Cat

Outline

This drama re-tells the story of the Good Samaritan (Luke 10:25-37), but using modern 'goodies' and 'baddies'.

A major problem with telling this parable today is that a 'Samaritan' is now a good person, whereas when Jesus told the story, a Samaritan was someone that you'd cross the road to avoid. A Jew would not help a Samaritan, and would certainly never expect to be helped by one.

That was the punch of the story, but it is lost today, because in our culture, the one supposed to be a 'baddie' is a helper, not a hooligan.

So this retelling uses an assumption of our time, that cats and dogs don't get on, and with that, the shock-value of Jesus' story returns. You can adapt this script for whatever animal puppet you have. There are suggestions for other combinations of 'goodies' and 'baddies' below.

You do not have to memorise these exact lines, since there are no cues for other actors. A story flows better when the story-teller uses their own words, so learn the gist and then extemporise if you wish.

Characters

- Narrator - person with Snuffles, a dog puppet

- optional: helper to move animal toys or pictures (no lines)

This script is written with cats and dogs, but you can adapt the story depending on the animal puppets you have. Here are some suggestions:

Farm animals version:

Sheep puppet
going to the field for his morning grass
gets chased into a thorn bush
by a wolf.
A cow, horse and donkey pass him by,
then he is rescued by another wolf
who gives him sweet, juicy daisies.
They played in the meadow all morning.

Jungle animals version:

Monkey puppet
going to his favourite banana tree
gets chased into a muddy swamp
by a lion.
An elephant, parrot and a hippo pass him by,
then he is rescued by another lion
who gives him crunchy, yummy monkey nuts.
They had fun climbing trees.

Sea creatures version:

Turtle puppet
going to a bank of seaweed for breakfast
gets chased into a swarm of stinging jellyfish
by a shark.
A dolphin, penguin and seahorse pass him by,
then he is rescued by another shark
who gives him sweet, juicy sea-cucumbers.
They went to play with the starfish.

Costumes & Props

Narrator will need a rolled-up bandage to wrap around Snuffles' head. It's a good idea to practise putting this on, as unrolling and tucking a bandage with one hand can be tricky!

All the other items mentioned, such as dog biscuits, can be mimed or can be real. The various animals can be mimed or can be toys or pictures.

Staging

I do this story by myself as Narrator, interacting with a puppet that I am holding. However, you could easily separate these parts and have one person act out the story with Snuffles, while a separate Narrator tells it.

Snuffles has no lines, but uses the 'whispering' technique, where he whispers to the Narrator when he wants to say something, and the Narrator repeats this to the audience. This is particularly effective if Snuffles appears to interrupt the Narrator occasionally.

The three dogs that pass by can simply be mimed, with Snuffles watching imaginary dogs walk across the stage. Alternatively, you can use pictures or soft toys, and have a helper move them from side to side as indicted in the script.

The Big Bad Cat can also be imagined. The Narrator can indicate with their spare hand how the Big Bad Cat pulled Snuffles' ears etc and how the other cat looked after him.

Alternatively, the helper can use cat pictures or toys to act out the story. Using the same cat for both characters (rather than a nasty-looking cat and a nice-looking cat) is important in getting the point across.

There are no lines for any of the animals, they just need to be moved as the Narrator tells the story.

The Narrator sits centre stage and tells the story. If you are using pictures or toys for the three animals that pass by, the first and third (poodle and dalmatian) start on the right side of the stage, and the second (sausage dog) on the left. Both cats start on the left.

If you don't have a helper, the Narrator can simply hold them up when needed.

Script

Snuffles and the Big Bad Cat

Narr: (throughout)

Hello everybody. I have a friend I'd like you to meet.
His name is Snuffles.

Would you like to meet Snuffles?
(yes)
Oh, you don't sound very sure.
Would you like to meet Snuffles?
(Yes!)

Oh, good. So, after three, let's all say "Hello Snuffles",
and we'll see if he will come out to meet you.
Ready? One, Two, Three!
(Hello Snuffles!)

[Snuffles enters]

Hello Snuffles!
This is Snuffles. He's my pet dog and he's …
[Snuffles whispers]
What's that Snuffles? You're feeling a bit shy?
[Snuffles nods, and continues to interact with Narrator
throughout]

Snuffles is feeling a bit shy, so he wants me to tell you
what he's saying.
Is that alright?
(yes)
So, what do you want to say to the boys and girls?
[whispering]
You want to tell the boys and girls a story?
That sounds good.

Would you like to hear Snuffles' story?
(Yes!)

What's your story about, Snuffles?
[whispering]
Ah. It's a story that Jesus told.
Jesus told a lot of good stories.
We can find his stories in The Bible.
I've got my Bible here.

[whispering]
And this story is called 'Snuffles and the Big Bad Cat.'
So is the story about you, Snuffles?
[nods]
That sounds good. So let us begin.
[Narr can pretend to read from Bible]

Jesus told a story to show us who we should be friends
with. He said:

Once upon a time, there was a dog called Snuffles ...
Hey that's you! ...
a dog called Snuffles who was going to the park to play
with his favourite ball when –
Oh No! He was chased by a Big Bad Cat!

[if using props, Big Bad Cat enters L and moves to
Snuffles, acting out the following, otherwise Narrator
acts it out.]

The Big Bad Cat pulled Snuffles' ears and bit his tail and
scratched his face and finally chased poor Snuffles into
a large bed of nettles and left him there.

[Big Bad Cat exits R]

Poor, poor Snuffles.
(ahhh)

It was worse than that.
(Ahhhhh!)

Poor Snuffles was so hurt that he could not get up. He just lay in the bed of nettles feeling very, very sad.
(Ahhhhh!)

But just then, a poodle came by. A fluffy white poodle.
[if using props, poodle enters R and crosses to L]

"Hooray!" thought Snuffles, "this fluffy white poodle will help me out of the nettles."

[Snuffles watches poodle (real or imaginary) cross stage]

But the poodle did not help Snuffles. She turned up her nose and walked straight past.

Oh. That wasn't very friendly. Poor Snuffles.
(Ahhhhh!)

But just then, a sausage dog came by. A long sausagey sausage dog.
[enters L and crosses to R]

"Hooray!" thought Snuffles, "this long sausagey sausage dog will help me out of the nettles."

[Snuffles watches sausage dog (real or imaginary) cross stage]

But the sausage dog did not help Snuffles. He looked the other way and walked straight past.

Oh. That wasn't very friendly. Poor Snuffles.
(Ahhhhh!)

But just then, a dalmatian came by. A big spotty dalmatian.
[enters R and crosses to L]

"Hooray!" thought Snuffles, "this big spotty dalmatian will help me out of the nettles."

[Snuffles watches dalmatian (real or imaginary) cross stage]

But the dalmatian did not help Snuffles. She turned her spotty back and walked straight past.

Oh. That wasn't very friendly. Poor Snuffles.
(Ahhhhh!)

Snuffles was feeling very sad. Would no-one come to help him?

Just then, someone else came along.
Was it the fluffy white poodle?
(no)
Was it the long sausagey sausage dog?
(no)
Was it the big spotty dalmatian?
(no)
Oh No! it was another Big Bad Cat!

[enters L and moves to Snuffles]

"Oh No!" thought Snuffles, "this Big Bad Cat will be mean to me. He will pull my ears
and bite my tail and scratch my face!"

[Snuffles shakes in fear]

But the Big Bad Cat did not do any of these things.
Instead, the Big Bad Cat pulled Snuffles out of the
nettles!

The Big Bad Cat found a bandage in his pocket,
(I didn't know that cats had pockets,
but apparently they do)
and he put the bandage around Snuffle's head.

[bandage head]

Then he rubbed Snuffles' ears better,
put some soothing cream on his tail,
and brushed his fur all smooth again.

Finally, the Big Bad Cat gave Snuffles his favourite treat -
dog biscuits!

Then Snuffles and the Big Bad Cat
(who wasn't bad after all)
went to the park to play ball together.

Two Men Praying

Outline

This drama tells the parable of the Pharisee and the Tax Collector (Luke 18:9-14), with the Narrator explaining the story to two puppets (or people), Rod and Andy.

Rod and Andy then act the story out, with Rod playing Mr Good-Stuff (the Pharisee) and Andy playing Mr Rubbish (the tax-collector).

The script features character from well-known children's films. Feel free to change the names to whatever characters are currently popular.

Characters

- Narrator - person
- Rod / Mr Good-Stuff - puppet
- Andy / Mr Rubbish - puppet

Costumes & Props

Narrator has clean handkerchief to give to Mr Rubbish, and uses a Bible to 'read' the story.

Rod / Mr Good-Stuff is dressed in posh clothes, such as a suit and tie. As Mr Good-Stuff, he swaggers and blusters.

Andy / Mr Rubbish is dressed in ordinary clothes. As Mr Rubbish, he has grubby handkerchief, and he droops and sighs.

Staging

The action happens centre stage. Rod and Andy start offstage and enter together. Then they exit and then re-enter to perform the play-within-a-play.

Narrator stands to one side, and can have a script on a lectern or clipboard.

Script

Two Men Praying

Narr:
[to audience]
Hello everyone. I've got a great story for you today.
Who would like to hear a story?
(Me! Me!)

[Rod and Andy enter]

Rod:
What? What was that?

Andy:
A story? Can we listen too?

Narr:
Of course you can. It's a story that Jesus told, about two men who went to pray. One was a Pharisee and the other a tax collector.

Rod:
A Who-isee?

Andy:
A What-alector?

Narr:
Oh I'm sorry. Let me explain. The Pharisees were people who were very, very careful to do everything right.

Rod:
Well, that sounds very good.

Narr:
And the tax collectors ... well they were *not* careful to do everything right. In fact, the one in our story did a lot of things wrong – a lot of, *lot of*, things wrong.

Andy:
Oh, dear. That wasn't good at all.

Narr:
You're right. It was rubbish

Can I get on with the story now?

Rod:
Yes, you can get on with the story now.

Narr:
Thank you. Ahem.
[pretending to read from a Bible]

Jesus told this story:

"Two men went up to the temple to pray, one a Pharisee, the other a tax collector.

"The Pharisee posed and prayed like this: 'Oh, God, I thank you that I am not like other people – robbers, crooks, cheats, or, heaven forbid, like this tax collector. I fast twice a week and give money to charity.'

"Meanwhile the tax collector, slumped in the shadows, his face in his hands, not daring to look up, said, 'God, have mercy. Forgive me, a sinner.'"

Jesus commented, "This tax collector, not the Pharisee, went home made right with God." (Luke 18:9-14)

Andy:
Huh? I don't get it.

Rod:
God was *not* pleased with the man who did all the *good* stuff?

Andy:
And God *was* pleased with the man who had done lots *wrong*?

Rod and Andy:
That can't be right!

Narr:
Hmmn, yes. I see why you're puzzled. I tell you what – let's act it out. Can you two help?

Rod:
Certainly. I'm classically trained, you know, Luvvie.

Andy:
Ooh, acting! I love acting! Can I be Lego Batman, please? Or Rapunzel? I do a really good Rapunzel, with my hair and everything and ...

Narr:
[interrupting]
No. There's no Rapunzel in our story. Or Lego Batman. Off you go and get ready.

[Rod and Andy exit]

Narr:
Once upon a time there were two men who went to pray.

One was a very good man who went to church every week and did a lot of good stuff. His name was Mr Good-Stuff. Here he is.

[Rod enters and stands to one side]

Rod:
[snooty voice]

I'm Mr Good-Stuff and I'm very, very, very, very, very GOOD!

Narr:
Yes, Mr Good-Stuff was very good. But he wasn't very wise. He thought that God would love him *because* of all the good stuff that he did.

Rod:
Yes. That's right. God loves me because of all the good stuff that I do.

Narr:
But that isn't right at all. Silly Mr Good-Stuff.

The other man was not good. He knew that he did rubbish stuff every day. His name was Mr Rubbish.

[Andy enters, hanging head, and stands to other side]

Andy:
I'm Mr Rubbish. Even though I want to do right, I end up doing wrong and it's all just so RUBBISH!

Narr:
Mr Rubbish did not feel happy. He knew that all the rubbish got between him and God. Poor Mr Rubbish.

Andy:
It's all just so RUBBISH!

Narr:
So there they were – Mr Good-Stuff and Mr Rubbish – and they both came to talk to God. Mr Good-Stuff prayed like this:

Rod:
Oh God, thank you that I am so good and such a nice person. I do lots and lots and lots of good things. You must be so pleased with me because of all the good

stuff that I do. Oh, what a good person I am.
Amen.

Narr:
Mr Rubbish, however, could not even lift his face up, but wept …
[Andy interrupts by blowing his nose loudly on the grubby hanky]

[louder] … he *wept* …
[Andy blows his nose again]

[even louder, looking at Andy]
… I said he **wept**

Andy:
Sorry.

Narr:
That's alright.

He wept because of all the rubbish things he had done.
He prayed like this:

Andy:
Dear God, I am so sorry for all the rubbish in my life.
Please forgive me and make me clean.
Amen.

Narr:
Now, Mr Good-Stuff thought that he never did anything wrong. How silly of Mr Good-Stuff. We all do rubbish things. We all need to say sorry – to people and to God.

Rod:
Oh, not me. I do lots and lots of good stuff, and God loves me because I'm so good.

Narr:

Oh dear. Silly Mr Good-stuff. God loves us because he is nice like that, not because of the good stuff we do.

So Mr Good-Stuff went home very happy with himself, but God was not so pleased.

[Rod exits]

Andy:

What about me?

Narr:

Ah yes, I'm just coming to you.

Mr Rubbish, however, knew that he did rubbish stuff, so he asked God to forgive him and help him to change.

And God, who loves to forgive, got rid of all the rubbish and wiped him clean.

God gave him a clean hanky
[takes away grubby hanky and gives Andy the clean hanky]
and a new name, Mr Clean.

Andy:

Ooh, I feel all clean inside now.

Narr:

So Mr Clean went home knowing that he and God were good friends.

[Andy does a little dance and exits]

Nasty Zac and the Cake-Fest

Outline

This sketch challenges the common assumption that we have to be nice before God will like us. Rod helps Andy to understand this by explaining about Zacchaeus – that Jesus knew all about Zacchaeus' dishonesty, and wanted to dine with him anyway (Luke 19:1-10).

This script uses British phrases that come in order; horse and cart, rhubarb and custard, Ant & Dec. If you are using the sketch in another country feel free to substitute alternatives.

Similarly, you can substitute coffee and doughnuts, or some other snack, if tea and cakes is too British.

Characters

- Rod - puppet
- Andy - puppet
- Reader - can be person from congregation

Andy is a bit of a twit.

Costumes & Props

Andy wears his t-shirt and hat backwards and is reading a Bible.

If you are using puppets, you can make a small Bible with several layers of folded paper and write Bible on the front, or have a real Bible on shelf by the theatre.

If you are using people, Andy could wear shorts and odd socks.

Staging

Andy is on stage at start, reading a Bible upside-down.

Script

Nasty Zac and the Cake-Fest

[Rod enters and turns Bible right way up]

Rod:
What'cha reading?

Andy:
I'm reading about Nasty Zac. It's one of my favourite stories.

Rod:
Who is Nasty Zac?

Andy:

He's the horrid little hairy dude who climbed a tree because Jesus didn't like him.

Rod:
Errrmmmm ... I think you mean ...

Andy:
And then he gave away loads of money, and then Jesus liked him.

Rod:
Errrmmmm ... that's not quite ...

Andy:
Yeah, he wanted Jesus to come round for tea and cakes and stuff but Jesus was all like, "Nah I won't, 'cos you're Nasty Zac and no-one likes you."

Rod:
Errrmmmm ... it's not like that ...

Andy:
But then Zac did some nice things and then he was Nice

Zac and Jesus was all like
"OK, I'll come round now, 'cos you've done something good, so I like you now."

Rod:
No, no, NO! It wasn't like that at all. You've got it all back to front.

Andy:
[turning around]
Back to front?

Rod:
Yes, you've got it the wrong way round.

Andy:
[looking at clothes]
What, my shirt? My hat?

Rod:
Well, yes, but that's not what I mean. You've got the story the wrong way round.

You've got the cart before the horse.
You've got the custard before the rhubarb.
You've got the Dec before the Ant.

Andy:
How do you mean?

Rod:
For a start, although Zac climbed a tree to see Jesus pass by, Jesus *wasn't going* to pass by, he was looking for Zac!

Andy:
Wozz-ee?
['Was he' said funny]

Rod:
Yes. And with the tea and cakes, Zac didn't invite Jesus round, it was all Jesus' idea.

Andy:
Wozz-it?

Rod:
And Jesus liked Zac waaaay before Zac gave back the money he'd taken. You were very wrong on that bit.

Andy:
Wozz-I?

Rod:
You certainly were.
Let's listen to how it really happened.

Reader:

> Then Jesus entered and walked through Jericho. There was a man there, his name Zacchaeus, the head tax man and quite rich.
>
> He wanted desperately to see Jesus, but the crowd was in his way – he was a short man and couldn't see over the crowd. So he ran on ahead and climbed up in a sycamore tree so he could see Jesus when he came by.
>
> When Jesus got to the tree, he looked up and said, "Zacchaeus, hurry down. Today is my day to be a guest in your home." Zacchaeus scrambled out of the tree, hardly believing his good luck, delighted to take Jesus home with him.
>
> Everyone who saw the incident was indignant and grumped, "What business does he have getting cozy with this crook?"

Zacchaeus just stood there, a little stunned. He stammered apologetically, "Master, I give away half my income to the poor – and if I'm caught cheating, I pay four times the damages."

Jesus said, "Today is salvation day in this home! Here he is: Zacchaeus, son of Abraham! For the Son of Man came to find and restore the lost." (Luke 19:1-10)

Andy:
Soooo … Jesus wanted to go and have tea and cakes with him, even when he was still Nasty Zac?

Rod:
Even when he was still Nasty Zac. Though I don't think that's really a good name.

Andy:
And Jesus knew what he was like? I mean, do you think maybe Jesus made a mistake and meant to go for tea with someone a bit nicer?

Rod:
No, he didn't make a mistake. I think Jesus was there looking for Zacchaeus, that's how come he knew his name.

Andy:
Oh yes! I see what you mean. But why would Jesus go and look for a crook?

Rod:
Jesus answered that one himself. He said he had come the find and restore the lost. And Zacchaeus was pretty lost!

Andy:
Yeah, he got lost up a tree!

But I still don't get it. Zac was a crook, yep?

Rod:
Yep.

Andy:
He took people's money, yep?

Rod:
Yep.

Andy:
And Jesus liked him, yep?

Rod:
Yep.

Andy:
Even before he did anything to deserve it?

Rod:
Yep.

Andy:
Soooo ... Does Jesus like me, even before I've done anything to deserve it?

Rod:
Yep! You've got it! You've finally got it!

Andy:
[starts to leave]
Brill! I'd better be off then. Loads to do!

Rod:
Where are you going in such a hurry?

Andy:
I need to bake some cakes and make some tea, and then find a sycamore tree to climb!

[exits]

Rod:
[sigh]
Every family tree has the odd nut!

[exits]

A *Real* Christian

Outline

This skit is fun way to think about what's important (and not) in our Christian faith. The idea is a game show, called 'Real Christian', in which the two hosts give a huge pile of unnecessary things to a bewildered new disciple.

The sketch requires a lot of props, but they will be to hand or hidden at the back of a vestry cupboard. You can use whatever props are appropriate for your church – robes, banners, kneelers – use whatever you can find.

Characters

- Chris - person
- Host 1 - person
- Host 2 - person

Hosts are game show presenters, and are brash and noisy. That have an annoying jingle for their show, Reeeeeeeeeeal Christian! They are all jazz hands and cheesy smiles.

Chris is nervous and overawed.

Costumes & Props

The hosts can wear flashy clothes, preferably matching. They carry clipboards, decorated with a logo of the 'Real Christian' game show, which hold lists of the items in their box.

Each host has a box of props containing alternate items listed in the script (adapt as necessary). For example:

> Large Bible and Bible reading notes
> 'Sunday clothes', eg suit and tie or dress and posh hat
> Sheaf of notice sheets
> Big dictionary and a lot of Christian books
> Load of CDs
> Hymn book (music edition)
> Guitar and load of music books
> Tea pot and tea towel
> Paper and scissors and coloured pens
> Frying pan, bacon and bread rolls
> Large old book
> Large candle
> Tambourine

Chris is dressed in ordinary clothes and sits in a swivel chair throughout, gradually being loaded up with the props.

Staging

The swivel chair is centre stage.

The boxes of props are set to left and right of the stage. The hosts' lists should match their props, in order from top to bottom of the box.

The hosts start off stage and enter to stand by the boxes. Each time a host speaks, they swivel Chris to face them, so that Chris gets spun round and round.

Chris starts off stage, possibly in the audience / congregation.

Script

A *Real* Christian

[Host 1 & Host 2 enter, and do a little dance to centre front]

Host 1:
Hello everybody …

Host 2:
and welcome to …

Host 1 & Host 2:
[with rising tone and jazz hands]
Reeeeeeeeeal Christian!

Host 1:
The show where we take an ordinary believer and turn them in to a

Host 1 & Host 2:
Reeeeeeeeeal Christian!

Host 2:
So without further ado, let's meet our lucky contestant. Who is it today?

Host 1:
Today's lucky contestant, and let's give them a great big …

Host 1 & Host 2:
Reeeeeeeeeal Christian!

Host 1:
… welcome, is … [looks at clipboard] Chris Tian! Come on up, Chris!
(applause)

[Chris enters]

Host 2:
Hello Chris, and welcome to the faith! Sit down and tell us a bit about yourself.

Chris:
[sits in swivel chair, facing front]
Thank you. Well, my name is Chri ...

Host 1:
Ha ha ha, That's a great anecdote. Thanks Chris.

Host 2:
And what is your big question today, Chris?

Chris:
Ummmn, well, I was wondering ...

Host 1:
[sidling in close]
Yeeeees?

Chris:
I was wondering ...

Host 2:
[sidling in close]
Yeeeees?

Chris:
I know that God loves me and I love God, but is there anything else I need to be a real Christian?

Host 1:
You mean a ...

Host 1 & Host 2:
Reeeeeeeeeal Christian!

Chris:
Oh, umm, yes, I suppose so.

Host 2:
[swivels Chris to face sideways]
Weeeell, I'm glad you asked that.

Of course, you need God –
the Lord Almighty,
the creator and saviour,
the comforter, friend and guide,
the mystery of the holy trinity,
the omnipresent, omnipotent triune majesty,
the divine paraclete,
Dominus dominantium,
Pater noster, qui es in caelis …

Chris:
[interrupting, looking confused]
But, but … How am I going to know all this?

Host 1:
[swivels Chris around to face the other way]
Weeeell, I'm glad you asked that.

Here's a guide book that gives you everything you need
to know.
[gives Chris a big Bible, preferable a huge lectern Bible]

Chris:
Great, thanks. So that's all I need?

Host 1:
You should probably have some notes as well so that
you don't just read your favourite bits.
[gives Chris some Bible notes]

[Chris gets swivelled around and around on each line
following]

Host 2:
But it would help if you wear the right clothes …
[gives Chris 'Sunday clothes']

Host 1:
And go to the right meetings ...
[gives Chris a sheaf of notice sheets]

Host 2:
And say all the right things ...
[gives Chris a big dictionary and a lot of Christian books]

Host 1:
And listen to the right music ...
[gives Chris a load of CDs]

Host 2:
And sing the right songs ...
[gives Chris a hymn book (music edition), guitar and load of music books]

Host 1:
And join the tea rota ...
[gives Chris a tea pot and tea towel]

Host 2:
And the Sunday school team ...
[gives Chris paper and scissors and coloured pens]

Host 1:
And the Saturday Morning Men's Prayer Breakfast Outreach Cooking Fellowship ...
[gives Chris a frying pan, bacon and bread rolls]

[swivel Chris to face the front. By this time Chris should be almost invisible under a pile of 'stuff']

Host 2:
[to Host 1]
Do you think we should throw in a prayer book and a candle, just to be sure?
[places a large, old book and large candle on top of the pile]

Host 1:
[to Host 2]
Yes, and a tambourine, to cover all eventualities.
[balances a tambourine on the top]

Host 1 & Host 2:
Now that's a Reeeeeeeeeeal Christian!
[high five and exit]

Chris:
[weakly, after a pause]
Help!

A Bad Friday

Outline

This poignant monologue makes a memorable Good Friday meditation. It is aimed at an adult or family audience, and has a quiet, reflective mood.

The speaker, a friend of the penitent thief, walks to Golgotha to be with his friend as he is executed. The speaker starts by recalling his experience of the previous Palm Sunday, then he meditates on prophecies of Jesus as he watches the procession on the Via Dolorosa. Finally, he describes the scene at Golgotha.

It is set in a modern reconstruction of Biblical times, as if the Bad Friday were happening today.

The script features Jer 23:5 & Zech 9:9 (quoted in Matt 21:5) and ends dramatically with the text of Luke 23:42.

Characters

- Speaker - person
- Thief - person (voice only, not on stage)

The speaker is a rough, working-class man from New Testament times. He is relating events from the first Good Friday, part narrating, part miming. The speaker does not have to adhere to the script exactly. It will flow better if he uses his own turns of phrase.

The thief does not appear on stage and has only one line, which can be spoken through the PA system.

Costumes & Props

Speaker is dressed in contemporary casual clothes. He needs a newspaper and a coat. Other props, such as a TV remote, can be mimed or real.

Staging

The monologue moves through three areas: home, street and Golgotha.

'Home' is at one side of the stage, and needs a chair with a coat hanging on the back, and possibly a table.

'Street' can be in the middle of the stage, or Speaker can walk slowly down a central aisle, depending on your PA capabilities.

'Golgotha' can be at the other side of the stage, or by a large cross or Easter garden, depending on the contents of the space. A small stool or box will help the speaker to remain visible while seated there.

Speaker starts sitting (possibly at a table) in the 'home' side of the stage, reading a newspaper.

The sketch may finish with a period of silence.

Script

A Bad Friday

Speaker: (throughout)

[sitting at table, puts down and folds paper as he speaks]

I was sitting, reading the paper, when my son yells from the other room.

[imitating son's voice]
"You've got to watch this! He's on TV!"
"Who is?", I ask.
"That guy everyone's talking about. They've got him on the news. It's just starting!"

[gets up from table and moves to doorway of 'other room' to look at TV, picking up remote if using prop]

So I turn up the volume and watch. I've heard the gossip – everyone has – about this fella with ideas above his station. But it makes good telly and gives us something to talk about.

Last week he staged a big parade in the city. It was all over the news. Made a right spectacle of himself, he did. It was all just a publicity stunt of course, and I bet the crowd was paid to be there.
[mocking]
'Hosanna this' and 'Hosanna that'. Still, it was more interesting than the footy.

[looks at TV]

So what's he doing now? It'd better be good, it's Sabbath this evening and I've got stuff to do.
[shaking head]
Na, it's just another parade? Seen that. Same old.
[about to turn away from TV]

I'm about to go when I see the 'hero of the hour' coming through the crowd.
[relating what the TV is showing]
But this isn't like last week. There's no red carpet, no paparazzi, no flag waving or autographs.

Instead it's all armed guards and a lot of shouting – nasty shouting.

The crowd parts and we see the 'Son of David' – that's what they call him ... [stepping back, looking shocked] ... oh.

[turns off TV with remote and returns to table]

I turn it off. I don't want my son to see this. There's enough violence without watching it on the telly too.

Why did they have to beat him up like that? Everyone loved him last week. But they went and arrested him anyway. And once you get on the wrong side of the State Security, well, that's where you end up. How did it get this way? Wasn't he supposed to be a king or something?

[sitting down again]

Of course, no-one believed it. We all had a bit of a laugh at him – I mean, he's from Nazareth, and we all know the nothing good comes from Nazareth. That's what my Mam used to say, anyway.

But I suppose I had this sneaking hope that maybe she was wrong. Might be nice to have a king like David back again, get rid of this flippin' State Security – bunch of filthy heathen!

[sits thoughtfully for a few seconds]

Anyway, I'd better get going. There's this bloke I have to see. I hate this kind of thing, but I'd better go. I promised his wife I would.

It's an old work mate of mine, you see. We did our apprenticeships together, but he was caught nicking stuff and got chucked, out and never made a straight penny since.

We've stayed mates, but ... he's more rough than diamond, you know?

[gets up from table, puts on coat]

Yeah. Anyhow. We both knew this day would come, and it's come today.

Friday. It's a bad Friday.

He's finally got his comeuppance, see? I can't say I'm surprised. Stupid idiot. He's had it coming for years, but it doesn't make it any easier.

I promised I'd go and be there at the end, but ... I kind of wish I hadn't now.

I call to my son.
"Just going out for a few hours. I'll be back before Sabbath."

[moves to centre stage, walking slowly on spot while talking, hands in pockets]

So I walk down the road. It's outside the city where they do … well, that's where it ends.

I meet the crowd I saw on the telly. They're going that way too, with the beat-up bloke from Nazareth. Might as well follow them, I guess.

[thinks to himself]

Y'know, they were reading some stuff at synagogue last week that made me think.
It was from the scroll of the prophet Jeremiah. How did it go now? Something like,

I will raise up for David a righteous Branch,
a King who will reign wisely
and do what is just and right in the land.
(Jer 23:5 NIV)

That'd make a nice change, I can tell you. And then there's that other bit,

See, your king comes to you, …
lowly and riding on a donkey.
(Zech 9:9 NIV)

Which prophet is that? I can never remember. Anyhow. I love that bit. Never understood it, but always loved it.

But it made me think. About the bloke. Last week. When he did that riding on a donkey thing and got his picture in all the papers, it reminded me.

"Hosanna to the Son of David", the crowd was yelling. And there he was, on a donkey – a donkey mark you –

and parading along like he was the fulfilment of all the Law and the Prophets!

Then he wonders why he gets into trouble with State Security!

[suddenly quiet, stops walking]

But, a donkey. Like whoever said. Was it just co-incidence?

It makes you think, doesn't it? The prophets. They couldn't really be talking about him …

… could they?

[resumes walking]

But it's daft. I mean, kings don't look like that, no king I've ever seen anyhow. And not like this poor wretch here, struggling along the road with his cross on his bleeding back, and the cameras licking up every juicy detail.

Looks like he's had quite a beating. What a mess.

And this crowd has certainly changed its tune, bunch of hypocrites! They ain't calling him a king now. Listen to 'em – huh!

[arrives at 'Golgotha', stops walking, looks to one side of main cross (real or imaginary)]

And so we arrive. They call this place 'The Skull'. Sounds about right. And I watch.

I try not to, but the horror somehow nails my eyes to the scene. There's my old mate getting himself spiked onto a Roman cross. Stupid, stupid moron! Why did you have to ...
[breaks off, close to tears]

Didn't you think of your wife? Your kids?
I catch his eye. We both look away, but I think he's glad I'm here.

[turns, looking to other side of cross]

And then they do some other poor sod. Doesn't look like there's anyone here to watch with him. Not a surprise. You're really on the scrapheap when you end up here. Even God doesn't look down on a hell-hole like this.

[turns to look to middle cross]

And then – him. The bloke from Nazareth. Pity really. He seemed like a nice guy.

My mate's a bit rough – put a few blokes in hospital – but this guy, by all accounts, healed people, even scum like Romans and Samaritans.

Dunno what he's done to deserve this, but that's the system for you.

[sits down on stool or box to wait]

They raise the crosses and drop them into the post-holes, each with a sickening thud
like the door of heaven slammed shut.

[pauses, cleaning nails]

And I wait to watch my mate die.

State Security pigs are playing dice. Nice. There's some women crying by that bloke from Nazareth, but that's about it.

It's like time has stopped, like the world is holding its breath, waiting for something to happen.

[looks to sky]
It's going to be Sabbath soon. I hope it doesn't take too long.

No, that didn't come out right. I meant for their sakes. They're the scum of the earth I know, but he's still my mate. And that one in the middle ... what's with him?

Never seen someone go so calmly to ... this. I don't even want to name it. It's supposed to be a sign of God's curse, isn't it?

[stands, angrily]

Then some idiots come from the town to laugh and throw insults at the dying.

[yelling at distant people]
Prats! Get a life!

That other bloke on the cross, not my mate, the other one, joins in the insults.

He's yelling at the Nazareth guy. Mocking him.

Seriously? You've gonna have them as your last words on this earth? Some people never learn.

[sits, and sighs]

Then my mate opens his mouth. He's nearly done, I can tell. I hope he has something better to say. This is his last chance before he meets Abraham, if that's where he's headed.

[looks towards first cross]
Please mate, for once in your life, make the right choice.

Thief:
[offstage]
Jesus, remember me when you come into your kingdom.

[pause, then exit]

Time Travel TV

Outline

This interactive drama retells the events of Holy Week. The Narrator doubles as a TV news anchor with reports from various scenes.

The drama can be split into sections with songs between for a family service, school play or family fun day. The audience has props to wave at appropriate times.

Characters

- Narrator - person
- Andy - puppet
- Rosy Parker - puppet
- Ian Keeper - puppet
- Joe - puppet
- Mary - puppet

The narrator doubles as a TV anchor. The five other characters can be separate people or puppets, or can be played by a minimum of three with costume changes. You will need a minimum of two puppeteers.

Costumes & Props

Narrator needs glasses to indicate the TV anchor, and a wobble board (a large sheet of card) to signal time travel. The audience / congregation can wobble in their seats and make a wobble noise as well.

Andy is a contemporary character and wears simple `casual clothes. A plain t-shirt is ideal so that it can be the basis for Joe if you are doubling up characters.

Rosy Parker is a TV reporter and can wear a plain dress, which can double later as robes for Mary.

Ian Keeper is a biblical innkeeper (like you hadn't guessed) and wears simple robes.

Joe is Joseph of Arimathea, so rich-man clothes would be appropriate. This can be the same puppet as Andy with a robe.

Mary can be played by the same puppet as Rosy with the addition of a head scarf and robe.

The audience have props to wave when indicated:

> palm leaves
> party plates
> wooden crosses
> stones

Make sure these are suitable for the age of audience, and distribute them either before or during the performance.

Staging

The puppet theatre is centre stage and Narrator stands to one side, with the wobble board nearby.

Narrator can use a lectern and read from script. This is particularly effective for the newsreader sections, where some appropriate paper shuffling and pressing a finger to the ear will aid the effect.

All puppet characters start off stage.

Script

Time Travel TV

Part 1 – Intro

[Andy enters]

Narr:
Hi Andy, you look a bit confused. What's the matter?

Andy:
Well, it's coming up to Easter, right?

Narr:
Right.

Andy:
And we're getting all excited about the chocolate and the eggs and the cute little chicks and everything, right?

Narr:
Right.

Andy:
And we have time off school and we get to have chocolate for breakfast and everything, right?

Narr:
Right. What's the problem?

Andy:
Well, what's it all about? And what's with the warm annoyed rabbits?

Narr:
The warm annoyed rabbits?

Andy:

Yeah, the hot cross bunnies! Why do we eat hot cross bunnies?

Narr:

Oh! Ha ha ha! I think you mean hot cross *buns*!

Well it just so happens that there's a TV program about to start which will tell us all about it. It's called Time Travel TV. Would you like to watch it with me?

Andy:

Yes please. And can the boys and girls watch too?

Narr:

Certainly. In fact, I'll need their help.
[to audience, showing props]
We have some things around so that you can join in with the story. We have palm leaves, party plates, wooden crosses and stones.

When you hear one of these mentioned in the story, you can pick it up and wave it. So listen out for the words. OK?

[Andy exits]

Narr:

Let's turn on the telly and get ready to watch Time Travel TV.

When we travel through time we will all go a bit wobbly, like this.
[wobble]
So get ready to travel through time with me.

- can break action at this point -

70

Part 2 – Palm Sunday

[Narrator puts on glasses to become TV anchor]

Narr:
[Wobble]
Good afternoon viewers and welcome to this edition of Time Travel TV.

The year is 33 A.D. Roman Emperor Tiberius Caesar is on the throne. The place is Jerusalem, and there are huge crowds waiting to see a famous celebrity.

[Rosy enters]

We cross to our roving reporter, Rosy Parker.
Rosy, what's that I can see in the background? Are they waving flags?

Rosy:
Not quite flags. The people in the crowd have got palm leaves from the trees and they are waving them in the air.

(Narr and audience wave palm leaves)

Some people have put their cloaks on the road to make a red carpet as well.

Narr:
So who is the celebrity, Rosy? I hear he is royalty.

Rosy:
The crowds are calling him The Son of David, our famous king, but he is actually a carpenter from Nazareth. His name is Jesus Josephson.

Oh, I see his procession coming into view. The crowds are waving their palm leaves.

(palm leaves)

I expect we'll see his special car soon, or perhaps he will be in a horse-drawn carriage. He's just coming around the corner.

Oh! He's *not* in a fancy car, or a carriage. He's riding on a donkey and he doesn't even have a crown. He doesn't look like any king I have seen.

But that's all from the parade with our carpenter king. Back to you in the studio.

[Rosy exits]

- can break action at this point -

Part 3 – Last Supper

Narr:
Thank you Rosy Parker, reporting to us from Palm Sunday. Now we will travel forward in time a few days, to the Thursday just before Easter.

[wobble]

It is a big party day in Jerusalem and we can talk to Mr Ian Keeper, who has rented out his room for a very special party.

[Ian enters]

Narr:
Good afternoon, Mr Keeper. I understand that the party is going on right now?

Ian:
Yes, it is. It's the Passover, see. That's the biggest party time of the year. We've got out all the best party plates.

(party plates)

Narr:
And who is at this party?

Ian:
Ah well. I'm glad you asked that. It's that celebrity who came to town last Sunday riding on a donkey. I was there, with my palm leaves,

(palm leaves)

and singing and waving, and now … here he is, with his friends, in my room! I'm so proud!

Narr:
They must be having a fun time

Ian:

I'm not sure about fun. They seem a bit quiet, actually. Not sad, but thoughtful.

They were eating bread and drinking wine and – not that I was listening at the door or anything – I thought I heard Jesus say he was going to die, and then come back to life again. But that's clearly daft. I must have heard wrong.

Narr:

Certainly that would be an amazing thing to do. Thank you, Mr Ian Keeper, for telling us all about The Last Supper. I'll let you go, so that you can wash up all the party plates now.

(party plates)

[Ian exits]

- can break action at this point -

Part 4 – Good Friday

Narr:
Now we will travel forward in time just one day, to Friday.
Our reporter, Rosy Parker, is back in the town square.

[wobble]

[Rosy enters]

Narr:
Rosy, it looks like there's a riot going on. Is it the crowd
with the palm leaves again?

(palm leaves)

Rosy:
No. The mood has changed a lot since last Sunday,
when the crowd were calling Jesus their king.

Now they are shouting for him to be killed. The Romans
have arrested him and put him on trial for his life.

Narr:
But why? What has he done wrong?

Rosy:
Nothing at all! Even the judge at his trial, Governor P.
Pilate, stated, "I find nothing wrong with this man." Yet
he has been sentenced to death anyway. And it is a
particularly nasty death. They will put him on a big cross
made of wood.

(cross)

Narr:
How dreadful. Has Jesus tried to escape this
punishment?

Rosy:
No, it is very strange. It's almost as though Jesus is
content to die. It's like he expected it.

Narr:
Strange indeed. Thank you Rosy.

[Rosy exits]

- can break action at this point –

Part 5 – Saturday

Narr:
Time-travelling another day brings us to Saturday.

[wobble]

It is a very sad day, and we can speak to Joe, a local landowner and friend of Jesus.

[Joe enters]

Narr:
Joe, can you tell us what happened yesterday, on Good Friday?

Joe:
Oh, it was terrible. Jesus died on that awful cross.

(cross)

But it was nearly night, so we buried him quickly in a cave, and closed the entrance with a huge stone.

(stone)

Narr:
That is very sad.

Joe:
Yes, but the worst bit is that we cannot visit Jesus' grave to bury him properly. We will have to do that tomorrow. Our friend Mary said she would help. Oh, here she comes now.

[Mary enters]

Narr:
Hello Mary. Joe said you are going to visit Jesus' grave tomorrow.

Mary:
Yes, I will go first thing tomorrow morning to put some spices on Jesus' body.

Narr:
That's kind. Perhaps I'll see you there on our next time travel. Good bye for now.

[Joe and Mary exit]

Narr:
Well. What a sad story. That was the first Good Friday. It doesn't sound very good, does it?

But this is not the end of the story. Let's time travel just one more day – to the very first Easter Sunday morning.

[wobble]

- can break action at this point -

Part 6 – Easter Day

[Mary Enters]

Mary:
Quick! Quick everyone! You'll never guess what just happened!

Narr:
Slow down Mary. What just happened?

Mary:
Ooooh! You'll never guess! You'll never guess!

Narr:
OK, so I'll never guess – you're going to have to tell me then.

Mary:
I've seen him!

Narr:
You've seen him?

Mary:
Yes, I've seen him!

Narr:
Who?

Mary:
Ooooh! You'll never guess! You'll never guess!

Narr:
OK, we've been through that before. Just tell me.

Mary:
Jesus! I've seen Jesus. He's alive.
He's really alive! He's really really really really really ...

Narr:
OK, I've got it. But what do you mean, you've seen him?

Mary:
I went to the grave early this morning to put some spices on Jesus' body, but when I got there the huge stone was rolled away!

(stone)

And there was an angel sat on top of it! He said that Jesus was alive!

Narr:
Wow!

Mary:
And then I ran off to tell everyone what I had seen, and I bumped into someone on my way. And guess who it was, you'll never guess! Come on, try to guess, you'll never guess!

Narr:
Was it ...

Mary:
It was Jesus! And he talked to me, and he told me to go tell everyone, so I'm going to tell everyone. They'll never guess! They'll never guess!

[Mary exits]

Narr:
Well, that is a happy ending to the story. Jesus did come back to life, just like he said.

That's all from Time Travel TV for today. Thanks for watching.

[Andy enters. Narrator removes glasses]

Andy:

Wow! So that's what Easter is all about! I'm really glad you put that program on. So is that why we eat hot cross buns at Easter?

Narr:

That's right, Andy. The cross reminds us of when Jesus died. He never did anything wrong, but when he died, he took the blame for all the wrong that I do, and that you do, that we all do.

And that means that we can be friends with God. And that is very Good News!

Andy:

Yay! So it really was a Good Friday after all!

30 Pieces of Chocolate (and a few more)

Outline

This script tells the story of the resurrection from Matthew 28, using chocolate bars to punctuate the script. It is great for a school service or assembly, or an Easter family service.

You could also use this script as an Easter fun day quiz. Print it out with _____ for the various bars, then have people try to fill in the gaps.

The chocolate bars listed are commonly available in the UK. If you have trouble sourcing them where you are, please feel free to amend as necessary.

Characters

- Hero - person

Hero is a Roman soldier reporting what happened on the first Easter morning.

Costumes & Props

Hero can wear a simple costume such as a cloak fastened at one shoulder or a helmet.

You will need a lot of chocolate for this sketch. The good news is you can give it away at the end of the service. Or you can eat it.

Staging

Have a table centre stage with the bars laid out in order. (You might like to label the bars with numbered stickers beforehand.)

Alternatively, eat the chocolate beforehand and stick the wrappers to a long piece of paper. The wrappers should be spaced out and in order. Then roll the paper up into a scroll and unroll it as you go through the script. Lining wallpaper is ideal for this.

You can encourage people to shout out the names as you hold the bars up.

Script

30 Pieces of Chocolate (and a few more)

Hero: (throughout)

Mornin'.
My name is Heronimus, legionnaire of the Imperial
Roman Army, but me mates call me Hero.

It all 'appened one Saturday night, sometime **After
Eight**, and me and my mate, **Freddo**, we was guarding
this tomb. "Guarding a tomb?" you say. Yeah that's a
Whole Nut of an idea, I know.

There was this guy, see. He'd been making trouble for
the guv'nor - reckoned he was **Divine** or summat - so
there was a **Bounty** on his head.

We'd given 'im a good **Walnut Whip**ping with **Kit-Kat**-'o-
nine-tails the day before, and executed 'im, but the
guv'nor sent us to make sure he stayed dead! No really,
I'm not **Lion**! You think that's mad? Join the **Club**!

Now my mate is a bit of a **Smartie**, so while we're stood,
guarding a dead body, he says, "Why don't we have a
Picnic?" And I thought, "Well, why not? I could do with
some **Time Out**."

So we sit down and we **Chomp** our sandwiches. I have
Creme Egg and cress sandwiches then I get all healthy
with some **Fruit and Nut,** (counts as two of your five-a
day!) and wash it all down with a nice big glass of **Dairy
Milk**.

Anyway, back on the **Topic**. After our food we was
Flaked out and ... well ... I'm not going to **Fudge** the
facts, we fell asleep. I know we shouldn't have, but we
did. We loosened our **Buttons**, pulled off our **Caramac**s,

and lay down under the **Milky Way**, counting all the **Stars** in the **Galaxy.**

Next thing I know, there's a **Crunchie** sound, like when you **Rolo** way a stone. I sat bolt upright and ... What **Kinder Surprise** was this! I couldn't have been more shocked if a **Penguin** had driven past in a **Double Decker**!

It was an angel – clothes all **Milky Bar** white, hair all **Ripple**y and **Curly Wurly** – just sat there, on top of the stone! And the tomb was open!

[open hollow egg]

Me and my mate, we was in a complete **Twirl** – we was so scared we called for our **Mars**! But just before we fainted clean away, we heard a heard a **Wispa** from the tomb, and someone stepped out, winked at me and said, "Morning, **Hero**!"

[faints]

Harvest from the Stars

Outline

This skit is great for a school assembly, or for a Harvest or Thanksgiving service. Andy wants to know where grapes come from, and Rod helps him to understand, both the supply chain and right back to creation.

The sketch lends itself well to interaction. You can ask the audience / congregation to answers Andy's questions, and they can have their own sticky note 'grapes' to add to the bunch at the end.

Characters

- Rod - person (needs to be able to click fingers)
- Andy - person or puppet

Costumes & Props

Rod needs green sticky notes, cut in circles or ovals, and marked with things we are saying 'thank you' for. We will use 10 in the drama, (atoms, stars, soil, grapes, farmers, sailors, truck drivers, warehouse workers, people on the supermarket checkout, you), but you may want to give one to each person present so that they can add their own thanks at the end.

You will also need a board or wall to put the sticky notes on, and a large bunch of green grapes.

Staging

Andy and Rod start off stage. There is a large bunch of grapes on the floor at one side. During the drama, Rod steps across the stage imagining 10 places to visually place the chain from God's 'click', through the grapes, to Andy.

The places are: Andy (1), supermarket (2), warehouse (3), truck (4), ship (5), farm (6), grapes (7), soil (8), stars (9), atoms (10).

You can have a small table for the grapes (7) at centre stage.

Script

Harvest from the Stars

[Andy enters]

Andy:
Ooooh grapes!
I really like grapes. I don't mind that they're on the floor, so ...
[holds grapes high above head and is about to eat them when Rod enters]

Rod:
Stop! You can't eat those grapes!

Andy:
Why can't I eat them? They look really yummy.

Rod:
You just found them on the floor.
You don't know where they've come from.
[takes grapes]

Andy:
Yes, I do. They've come from the floor.

Rod:
No, I mean before that.

Andy:
Well before that they came ...
Oh I get it.
This is Harvest, right? We're supposed to say that they came from God.
And 'Thank you God for the grapes' and all that, yes?

Rod:
Well, yes, I suppose so.

But I was more thinking that it's not good to eat stuff you've found on the ...

Andy:
[not really listening]
But ... they don't really.

Rod:
They don't what?

Andy:
They don't come from God.
Grapes come from Tesco's.
(substitute supermarket of your choice)

Rod:
That's true. Grapes do come from supermarkets.
So we can thank God for supermarkets and all the lovely food ...

Andy:
[not really listening]
How?

Rod:
How?

Andy:
Yes, how? Grapes come from supermarkets, but how?
Do they have big grape plants in the fruit and veg aisle?
[wiggles hand upwards for growing plant]

Rod:
No, they don't have big grape plants in the fruit and veg aisle.
[steps sideways to place (2) and wiggles hand upwards for growing plant]

Andy:
So where do grapes come from before the

supermarket?
(I know where they go to afterwards – my tummy!)

Rod:
You want to know where grapes come from before the
supermarket?
That's a very good question.
They come from a big warehouse.
[steps sideways to place (3) and mimes stacking boxes]
And they get there in a lorry.
[steps sideways to place (4) and mimes lorry]

Andy:
And where do they come from before that?

Rod:
They come in huge ships from sunny countries where
they grow grapes.
[steps sideways to place (5) and mimes ship]

Andy:
And where do they come from before that?

Rod:
They don't come from anywhere before, they grow
there, on a grape farm.
[steps sideways to place (6) and mimes farm]

[indicating supply chain from farm to tummy]
And lots of people farm them and sail them and drive
them and stack them and sell them …

Andy:
And I eat them!

But … where do they come from before that?

Rod:
I've told you. They don't come from anywhere. They
grow here, on the grape farm.

[steps sideways to place (7) and places grapes on table, centre stage]

Andy:
But they must come from somewhere. You can't just magic nothing into a grape. Where does all the juicy juice inside a grape come from?

Rod:
Well, I suppose the juicy juice comes from the water that the farmer gives to the plant.

Andy:
And what about all the grapey bit that keeps the juicy bit in?

Rod:
That comes from all the goodness in the soil.
[steps sideways to place (8) and mimes soil]

Andy:
Grapes are made from soil?

Rod:
Well, yes.
Everything in this world is made from other things. You are made from grapes! Your body breaks down the grapes into all the little molecules and atoms, and then rearranges them to make you. It's rather clever.

Andy:
So I come from recycled grapes?

Rod:
Yup.

Andy:
Cool!
And grapes come from recycled soil ... and soil comes from ...

Rod:
Well, ultimately, recycled stars!
[steps sideways to place (9) and mimes stars]

All the atoms that make up everything in the world –
grapes and trucks and supermarkets, even you – all
those came, billions of years ago, from massive
exploding supernovas!

Andy:
Awesome!
And where do they come from before that?

Rod:
Before that?

Andy:
Yes, where do the atoms and stuff all come from, right
at the start. They must come from somewhere.

Rod:
Hmmn. That's one's a bit tricky, because there wasn't
anyone around then to see, but we think it probably all
started with everything exploding from nothing in a
really, really, really big bang!

Andy:
[with an air of 'I've heard that before']
Oh. I thought you were going to say something all big
and sciencey.
I've read about that in the Bible. When God went …
[tries to click fingers]
When God went …
When God went …

Rod:
[steps sideways to place (10) and clicks]
You mean when God went [click] and then there was
everything?

Andy:

Yup. That's it.

And the [Rod clicks] made the atoms, and the atoms made the stars, and the stars made the soil, and the soil made the grapes, and the grapes made me!

Rod:

That's right. So when we say thank you for grapes we can say thank you for all these things as well:

[walking back along the ten places, miming them as each is said. Either Rod or someone else can stick the grapes on a board to make the bunch]

For atoms (10)

[clicks and sticks 'atoms' sticky note at bottom of board]

For stars (9)

[mimes stars and adds 'stars' sticky note, building up a bunch of grapes]

For soil (8)

[mime soil etc]

For grapes (7)

[eat one]

For farmers (6)

For sailors (5)

For truck drivers (4)

For warehouse workers (3)

For people on the supermarket checkout (2)

For you (1)

So where do grapes come from? The same place as you and me – [click].

NaTVT 4 U
The Christmas story in TXTSPK

Outline

In this sketch, two angels receive text messages from God, which tell the story of the first Christmas using text abbreviations.

Feel free to replace 'Dr Who' with whichever TV show is trending.

Characters

- Angel 1 - person or puppet
- Angel 2 - person or puppet
- TXT - God's text messages

Costumes & Props

Angels can be in robes or in modern dress with tinsel halos.

Both angels need over-sized mobile phones. If you are using people, these can be clipboards decorated on the back to make them look like mobile phones. The angels can then have their lines on the clipboards. If possible, make all the lines fit on a single page.

If you are using puppets, real mobiles are the right size. Put them on stands or attach them to sticks with rubber-bands.

Text messages can be printed out (at least A3 size) and held up at the right time, or projected, so that the congregation can read them.

Staging

You will need a sound effect for a text message coming in. You can play a ringtone though a mic, or have the congregation say 'buzz' by the same method as you use for the messages. It is indicated in the script by [buzz].

Angel 1 starts off stage, mobile phone in use.

Angel 2 starts centre stage ostentatiously praying, mobile phone hidden.

Script

NaTVT 4 U –
The Christmas story in TXTSPK

[Angel 1 enters texting on phone. Angel 2 looks shocked.]

Angel 1:
[looking innocent]
What?

Angel 2:
You're on your phone? In heaven?

Angel 1:
So?
[to audience]
There's great reception here.

Angel 2:
Yeah, I know.
[brings out own phone]
What'cha looking at anyway?

Angel 1:
It's a message from the boss. He says he's going down.

Angel 2:
[in naff rap style]
What, you mean ...
going down wiv da bros,
do ya know what I mean?
'Cos he's diggin' the scene.

[getting stuck for a rhyme]
He's the Lion of Judah,
he's never very rude-ah.

[slowing down]
A hip chillin' master who's ...
got a sticking plaster ...?

... umm ... yo?
[pose]

Angel 1:
[giving Angel 2 a weird look]
No. He's says he's going down ... there.
[points down to earth]

Read it for yourself.
[shows phone]

TXT:
[projected onto a screen or written on large cards for
congregation to read]
lol 2 ppl
cul8r

Angel 2:
[Reading phone and trying to pronounce it like words]

lol-two-puhpul-culayter?
Lol Two Puhpul? God's got two lollies and they're
purple?

Angel 1:
No, no, no. It's text-speak. You have to say the letters,
and they're short for things.
Like the cu, it means 'see you', you see?

Angel 2:
Oh, I get it now. God and his modern tech, eh?

Ooh. LOL, I think I've heard of that one. Laughing Out Loud, isn't it? Or it might mean Lots Of love. Or it could be Little Old Lady. Is it Little Old Lady?

Angel 1:
No. It's not Little Old Lady. You forgot Lord of Lords.

Angel 2:
Oh yes. Lord of Lords.
[embarrassed laughter]

Ummn I don't get the rest.
[asks congregation / audience for help]

[enlightened]
Ahhh, Lord of Lords to people, see you later.

[confused]
Er, 'see you later'? Does that mean that God's going away?

Angel 1:
No, don't worry. He's got that omnipresence thing.

[Angel 2 still looks confused]
He's still up here, even when he's down there.

Angel 2:
Oh, OK. I see. I think.
[mumbling to self]
Never did get that whole omni-watsit.

[buzz]

Angel 1:
Hey! Another text has come in. Look!

TXT:
PPP 2 ppl
plz fwd

Angel 2:
What?
[asks congregation / audience for help]

Oooooh, peace to people. I get it. Clever!

Angel 1:
It also says, 'please forward'. I think we're supposed to pass it on.

[calling off stage]
Hey, guys, is anyone nipping down to earth soon?
[pause, waiting for 'reply']

You are, Gabriel?
Great, could you take this message for us please?
[show phone, then pause, waiting for 'reply']

Who to? Oh, ummn, well he just said 'to people', so anyone you meet, I guess. In the supermarket or down the pub or ...
[pause, waiting for 'reply']

Oh, you were just going to abide in a field? That's fine. I'm sure you'll find someone there.

[buzz]

Angel 2:
Oh, oh! Another text has come in. What's this one?

TXT:
lol <3 ppl
want 2 b bff
doing f2f 4 ne1
cos wysiwyg

Angel 2:
I really don't get this. Can you text him back and ask him to be a bit clearer?

[Angel 1 sends text]

[to audience]
Can you help me?

[as audience helps]
'Lord of Lords loves people' – yep, that's true enough.

'Want to be best friends for ever'.
Wow, that's amazing – they get to be friends with the boss! Is that like facebook friends? I wonder if God is going to 'like' them?

Angel 1:
I think it's even better than facebook friends. I've heard he's wanting to adopt daughters and sons.

Angel 2:
Awesome! But I don't get the rest of the message. How would God do a 'face to face for anyone'? And it's one thing saying, 'what you see is what you get', but how are people going to see God?

[buzz]

Angel 1:
Ah, I've got a reply to your text.

Angel 2:
My text?

Angel 1:
Yes, when you asked God to be a bit clearer. The boss says he *is* being clearer. In fact, he's doing it right now, so that everyone can understand. He says we should look down and see what's happening.

Angel 2:
What, now?

Angel 1:
Yes, right now.

Angel 2:
[on phone]
OK, hang on a minute while I get Google maps up …
hang on, it's just loading …
[making forward circling motion with finger]
… still loading …

Angel 1:
[arms folded]
Is it slow because you're using up half of heaven's
bandwidth streaming back-to-back Dr Who again?

Angel 2:
[looking sheepish]
Yeah, sorry. Oh, it's up now. Where should I look? And
When?

Angel 1:
He says it's in the Roman Empire, in the time of King
Herod. Look for an odd little corner called Judea.

Angel 2:
Ummn, er, yep got it. Yeesh – it doesn't look like they've
exactly got fibre-optic there! Why ever would God want
to bother with that tiny place?

Angel 1:
Ah well, you know the boss. 'Every hair on their heads is
numbered', and all that.

Can you zoom in? There's a town called Bethlehem.
Apparently, there's an inn with a back room.

Angel 2:
An inn? There's dozens! Which one does he mean?

Angel 1:
Well I don't know, do I? The boss just said to look. Try going into street view.

Angel 2:
Oh yeah. Umnn, how about … oh, I think I've found the one. There's a bunch of shepherds heading that way. And I can see Gabe hanging around.

Angel 1:
Zoom in. Closer. Closer.
[leaning in to look at screen]

Angel 2:
Oh, it's good innit? It's just like being there – you can see right inside!

Angel 1:
What's that in the box in the corner?
[squinting at phone]
Looks like a baby! Surely that can't be …

Angel 2:
I think it is! It really is …
[looking closer]

[buzz]

TXT:
4 u irl
with lol from lol

Angel 1:
For you, in real life

Angel 2:
with lots of love from Lord of Lords

[buzz]

TXT
OMG

Both:
[bowing with reverence]
Oh, My God!

Bold, Frankenstein and Mmmm-errr

Outline

This sketch reveals the original story about the three wise men, and shows the gifts they *really* brought to Jesus. (Matthew 2:1-12)

Characters

- Narrator - person
- Balthazar - person or puppet
- Melchior - person or puppet
- Gaspar - person or puppet

Gaspar is a lovable twit.

This script was originally played by just two people. The version here can be played by two, three or four people, or one person and three puppets (minimum of two puppeteers).

For two people:

> One actor is Narrator and the other plays all three wise men, with three hats and three accents. This option uses the *section in italics*.

For three people:

> Two actors play Balthazar and Melchior respectively, with the third doubling as Narrator and Gaspar. In this case Narrator should stand to one side at a lectern when narrating, then step

into the action and add a hat to play Gaspar. This option omits the *section in italics*.

For four people, or one person and three puppets:

One person is the Narrator, and the other three people or puppets are the wise men. Omit the *section in italics*.

Costumes & Props

The three wise men need fancy headgear. For example, a crown, mortarboard, 'boffin' wig or jewelled turban (wrap fabric around the base of a fez and add a brooch). Gaspar can have something silly, such as a fairy princess tiara or a baseball cap with 'I'm clever' written on it.

Balthazar can have a telescope. Melchior needs a celebrity gossip magazine.

The Narrator has the three gifts initially and gives them to the wise men where indicated. All three gifts are conceqaled, either under cloths, wrapped in paper, or in boxes.

Balthazar's gift is Bold laundry detergent.

Melchior's gift is a Frankenstein toy or mask.

Gaspar's gift is the 'Mmmm-errr', a weird, heart-shaped construction of pipe-cleaners, feathers, glitter etc. It's the kind of thing your pre-schooler would bring home and you'd say, "That's lovely dear, what is it?"

The Mmmm-errr needs a hanging loop so that the Narrator can hang it on a Christmas tree or over a manger towards the end of the sketch.

Staging

The narrator stands to one side with the script on a lectern. If you are using puppets, the theatre is centre stage.

Balthazar, Melchior and Gaspar start offstage and all enter from the same side.

When 'riding camels', all three move around the stage, church or hall in a line (in Monty Python horse-riding style). Gaspar is at the back.

If there is a nativity scene in a suitable place, the wise men can end their journey there and present their gifts towards the manger.

Script

Bold, Frankenstein and Mmmm-errr

Narr:

A long time ago, in a galaxy far, far away ...
Oh hang on, wrong story. That's Star Wars. We don't
have any wars in this story, but there is a star. Let me
start again ...

A long time ago, in a desert far, far away there were
three wise men. Sometimes we call them kings or magi
but really, they were scientists.

[Bal enters, looking at the sky and measuring their
positions with his hands]

They studied the stars, and plotted the planets, and
measured the meteors. And one night they saw
something very special ...

Bal:

Wow! Look at that amazingly bright star up there!
[calling offstage]
Melchior, Gaspar, come and look!

[Mel enters, if this is played by the same person, swap
hats and turn to face the opposite way]

Mel:

What is it, Balthazar? What have you seen?

Bal:

Look Melchior. Look up there. It's a super nova, I think.

> *(This section only when using two actors)*
>
> **Narr:**
> *[interrupting]*
> *Hold on a minute. What's going on here? I said*

there were three wise men. Are you playing all of them?

Bal:
Yes, well, budget cuts, you know. And Colin Firth was busy and had to cancel.

Narr:
Hmmn, OK then. I suppose it'll have to do. Get on with the story.

Bal:
Where was I? Oh yes. Look up there. It's a super nova, I think.

What do you reckon Gaspar? Gaspar?

[looking round]
Where's Gaspar?

Mel:
I don't know. He's probably messing around making something sticky, as usual.

A super nova you say? I think you're right.

[aside to audience]
But since the scientific terminology won't be invented for the best part of two thousand years, we're a bit ahead of our time here.

Bal:
What could it mean?

Mel:
Well, I've been looking through my guide to the stars
[holds up celebrity magazine]
and it says that a new star means a new king!

Bal:
A new king? That's amazing! We should go and visit him.

We could take gifts too – something useful would be good.

Mel:
Or the latest toy – something every kid would want.

Bal:
Brilliant! That's all settled then. Meet you by the camels in half an hour!

Gas:
[puffing]
Sorry I'm late guys, I was just making … mmmm-errr … well, something. What have I missed?

Mel:
Only the biggest news of the century! We're going to find a new king, and take him gifts.

[reluctantly]
I suppose you had better come too. Make sure you bring a present for the new king,
and make sure it's good, not your usual home-made rubbish.

What have you been making anyway? Did you know you've got glue on your nose?

Gas:
Mmmm-errr, it's … ummm, I'm not sure really.

Mel/Bal:
[shaking heads]
Oh, Gaspar!

Narr:
So the three wise men packed their pyjamas and their tooth brushes, and went on a long journey to find the new king. They took presents with them too.

[giving the gifts to the kings in turn]

Balthazar took a very useful present.
Melchior took the latest new toy.
And Gaspar ... well Gaspar hadn't really had much time to get anything ready, so he just grabbed some bits and bobs from his craft bench where he'd been making the ... mmmm-errr ... something.

[Wise Men riding on camels. Gaspar is fiddling with his present]

Bal:
Urgh, I hate long journeys. These camels really give me the hump.

Mel:
Me too. And I'm hungry. Is there anything to eat?

Bal:
Sorry, no. There's nothing but the sandwiches all around us.

Mel:
Bother. And no dessert either I suppose?

[looking round, grumpily]
What's Gaspar messing around with back there?

Bal:
I don't know. He's done nothing but fiddle, fiddle, fiddle since we left. Hey, Gaspar, what are you making?

Gas:
Mmmm-errr, well, it's sort of ... I'm not sure what it's called, but it's going to be good. (I think).

Mel/Bal:
Oh, Gaspar!

Narr:

After many days of riding, a few wrong turns and an argument over the sat nav, eventually the three wise men reached their destination.

It was not a palace, as they had expected, just an ordinary house. The mum and the dad were not a queen and a king, just ordinary people. The new baby was not wearing a crown, just ordinary baby clothes.

But still, Balthazar, Melchior and Gaspar knew that this baby would grow up to be the King of Kings.

Bal:

[importantly]
Since I was the one who first saw the star, I should be the first one to give my gift to the new king. I have brought the best gift after all. A very practical gift.

[holds out gift, still concealed]

I have brought a very large tub of the best quality washing powder – the finest that money can buy. The new king will think that my gift is the best!

Mel:

[elbowing Bal out of the way]
No no! My gift is far better! I have been round all the shops and have the very latest fashionable toy.

[holds out gift still concealed]

Every kid wants one, and it cost a packet, I can tell you! The new king will think that my gift is the best!

What about you, Gaspar? You're being very quiet. What have you brought?

Gas:

Mmmm-errr, I don't really know what you'd call it.

[looks at gift in furtive manner, keeping it hidden]
But I have been working on it very hard.

Mel/Bal:
Oh, Gaspar!

Narr:
So the three wise men knelt before the new king, and presented their gifts:
[each reveals gift, holding it high so that everyone can see, then kneels]

Bold,

Frankenstein,

and Mmmm-errr

Mary said thank you for the toy and the washing powder, and treasured them away for later on – like when someone got around to inventing a washing machine, but the Mmmm-errr she took and hung above baby Jesus.

[Narr hangs Mmmm-errr on tree or above crib if one is handy]

And Jesus looked at the Mmmm-errr, and knew that Gaspar had made it, not with glitter and pipe-cleaners, but with time, with care, and with lots of love. And that made it the best present of all.

[moves to centre stage]

And that's why we have Christmas; because God sent Jesus to live with us, to spend time, care, and lots of love on us. And that makes Jesus the best present of all.

Using Drama in (and out of) Church

Practicalities

It's a rare luxury in school and church drama to have a troupe of talented actors, with oodles of rehearsal time, a purpose-built theatre and a whole wardrobe department, not to mention make-up, scenery and props – so rare that I've never had it.

Instead, it might be down to you and one other person, and perhaps a third who has had their arm twisted and would rather not speak, with whatever props you could find at home.

Sound familiar? Then you'll find these scripts reassuringly accessible.

All of the sketches have minimal requirements for props and costumes, and many can be performed by one or two people, with little rehearsal. Of course, being more polished and slick is better, but if you find yourself in a last-minute panic, fear not!

Lines!

It is best if everyone knows their lines by heart, but this is not always practical, particularly with narrators, who may have a lot of words.

If you have short preparation time, then avoid stumbling over words by letting performers have their words on a prop. Several scripts have clipboards for just this purpose, although actors should use these as *aides memoire*, rather than visibly reading the words.

Another way around needing to learn words is to use puppets and a puppet theatre, so that the performers are hidden and can read from scripts attached just below stage level. If there is more than one puppeteer, have several copies, so that everyone has all the pages in easy sight.

Costumes

Basic costumes can help the audience to identify characters, for puppets as well as to people. It need only be a hat or a cloak or a prop. There are suggestions in the scripts, but feel free to adapt or ignore as you wish.

It can be effective to mix Biblical and modern clothing. For example, an angel could wear hoodie and jeans plus a tinsel halo, or long flowing (choir?) robes plus headphones and trainers; Elijah could wear long biblical robes (charity shop curtains?) and carry a Filofax or ring binder.

Can You Hear Me, Mother?

If you are using a puppet theatre, or if you are performing outdoors, you will probably need some form of amplification. Both fabric and open air dissipate sound very quickly, and even the best speaker can find their voice lost.

Simple tie-clip mics work very well, although puppeteers need to make sure they do not 'ruffle' the mic backstage. You can also fix a boom stand horizontally, and use an omni-directional mic. This can pick up all the speakers well, but is only practical when using a larger puppet theatre, such as the plastic-pipe design, described below.

People and Puppets

Most of these dramas will work with people or puppets or a combination of both. You can cast people in parts suggested for puppets, but not always the other way around if the character uses props.

It is often easier to recruit puppeteers than actors, and characterisation is usually simpler with puppets. For example, a child can usually work a puppet dressed as an old person or a baddie more convincingly than playing the character themselves.

One puppeteer can work two puppets at once, and this can be helpful for synchronising conversations, such as in 'Elijah and the Ravens'. Larger puppets with moving mouths are visibly more dynamic than glove puppets and are more effective in maintaining the illusion of life. Feel free to substitute animals or monsters for people, and to swap male and female characters where appropriate.

You can combine people with puppets very easily. A narrator can stand beside a puppet theatre and interact with the puppets, or a human character can be inside the theatre with their shoulders at stage level. If you prefer not to have a theatre, you can hold a puppet as if it is sitting on your knee and talk to it as a person.

But I Can't Throw My Voice!

Neither can I. Using puppets in drama is about communicating in an appealing and accessible way, not ventriloquism.

There are three main ways of making a puppet 'talk' without resorting to 'a gottle of geer'. The first is to be hidden behind a theatre and simply talk, moving the puppet in time. If you are using a moving-mouth puppet, remember to *open* the mouth on each syllable, not shut it!

If you are visible while operating your puppet, a simple method is to use whispering. The puppet whispers to you, and you repeat the words to the audience. You'll find this in 'Snuffles and the Big Bad Cat'.

But often, I simply speak the words for the puppet, in a voice different from my own, and move the puppet animatedly with the words. It is amazing how effectively a moving mouth, synchronised with sound, gives the impression that it is the puppet talking, not me.

Puppet Theatres

If you are using puppets, a simple theatre is very useful. It helps to maintain the illusion of the puppet world, and does away with the need to learn lines, because you can have the script pinned or stuck to the inside. A theatre also allows you to set the scene with simple backgrounds. These can be pictures pinned or stuck to the theatre.

Remember that voices carry less well from behind a theatre, so make sure you e-nun-ci-ate!

Height

Theatres should be as low as is convenient, to be more in contact with an audience mainly of children, but high enough to hide the puppeteers without giving them permanent stoop! You have three choices: puppeteers standing, kneeling or sitting.

- Standing makes it easy for the puppeteers to move around, but is a long way up for the audience.

- Kneeling is a good compromise between viewing height and manoeuvrability, but older people may find it difficult to move around on their knees.

- Sitting on the floor makes the stage closest to the audience, but means that puppeteers cannot move.

Once you have chosen your height, there are various ways to construct a theatre, either temporary or re-usable. There is the classic cardboard-box-with-a-window, but if you need some ideas, try one of these:

Washing Line

Stretch a cord at a suitable height across the stage area, attaching it firmly to whatever tables, pillars, lecterns or pulpits are available. Make sure that the line is taut and does not dip too much in the middle.

Drape sheets or light blankets (fleece is good) over the cord. If you are in a traditional church building, be aware that backlighting from a large East window can make puppeteers visible through light fabrics.

Table

Folding tables make great temporary puppet theatres, but they are quite low, so are better suited to children, and even then they will have to sit on the floor.

A small GoPak-style table will fit one or two people, while the large size will fit two or three. You can use the table surface for titles or scenery.

Lie the table on its side with the legs out, and drape the legs with sheets if you want to remain hidden from the sides. If the table feels like it might tip over, add weights to the ends of the legs (kneelers or old hymn books are ideal).

Chair

For the simplest of all theatres, place a chair with its back towards the audience and kneel at the side, resting your elbow on the seat. The puppet will appear over the top of the back and you can interact with it from the side.

Depending on the dimensions, you might want to put some old hymn books (they're so useful!) on the seat to raise your puppet to the right height. If the back of the chair is not solid, drape some cloth over to hide your elbow.

Shower Rail

If you have a doorway or an archway, you can use an expanding shower rail with a curtain or sheet to make a theatre of any height. You need the type of rail that is spring-loaded and attaches by pressure between the walls.

You can even have opening curtains (woo hoo!) by using a second pole further up. Cut the bottom half off a shower curtain and drape this over the lower pole, securing it with stitching or double-sided sticky tape (check what sticks to your curtain).

Cut the top half into two and hang each from the upper pole with the curtain rings.

Canes

Use bamboo canes to make a free-standing frame at any height, and of any size or shape. Attach the canes with rubber bands or tape to microphone stands, easels, lecterns or whatever stands you have available. Old-fashioned clothes horses make instant frames, too.

Add blankets, sheets or duvet covers to make a brightly-coloured theatre. You can secure the fabric with colourful pegs, and leave them showing as part of the design.

Banner

Use thick fabric to make a large rectangle with a rectangle cut-out for the stage. Curtain material works well for this, and is easily sourced from a charity shop. Use a broomstick-sized pole to support the banner, and add dowels or dress stiffening above and below the cut-out to maintain the shape.

Hang the banner from whatever hooks or fixtures you have available, such as the curtain rail of a bay window, or between tall cupboards. This type of theatre rolls up easily for storage and can be used at standing, kneeling or sitting height. If you make a shorter banner and need it longer, you can simply pin a cloth at the bottom.

Plastic Pipes

I have a semi-permanent theatre made from the plastic piping used for plumbing sinks. It is light, transportable and adaptable for myriad uses. The theatre is made from a zig-zag of rectangular frames with fabric drapes.

You will need at least two frames so that it can stand up, but three or four frames are (literally) more flexible. I have one set at standing height and another at kneeling height. The taller can be used as a background for the shorter, or they each can be used alone. I have also used them for scenery and wings for drama.

The piping comes in black, white or grey, in several sizes, and with various systems for joining. I used black 40mm pipes. I do not recommend the narrow-bore pipes because these are likely to bend in use.

For each frame, use four 90° bends and enough pipe to fit the perimeter of your rectangle. Make sure that your frame is flat and square by assembling it on the floor.

Fix the joints solidly so that they cannot twist once you have assembled the frames. I used hot glue. Join adjacent frames with three or four long plastic cable ties. This will let you fold the frames to different shapes and concertina them for storage.

The fabric panels can be flat or gathered. Mine simply drape over the frames with fabric on both sides to balance the weight. I have one side black and the other brightly coloured. I added velcro strips to make sure nothing moves.

The Stuff at the Back

About the Author

Hi! I'm Fay.

In no particular order I am a mum, maths lecturer (more letters *after* my name than *in* my name!), author, blogger, knitter, theology student, children's worker and mad scientist.

Sources close to the author (who wish to retain anonymity in the interests of national security) report that "Fay would out-tigger Tigger for energy and enthusiasm". I say nothing to deny or confirm.

I write The Reflectionary (www.reflectionary.org), a weekly blog of lectionary-based resources for churches, youth-groups, children's work and schools' ministry. Popular items are the crafts, all-age worship materials, the printables and the scripts.

I'm also a theology student – Woo Hoo! I'm studying Theology, Ministry and Mission at Wesley House, Cambridge. If you want to follow my life there, you can visit www.anewfayz.wordpress.com.

This all started when I was in church, hearing Luke 9:59 (Jesus' conversation with a young man making excuses for not following). It hit me round the head like a rolled-up newspaper, wielded with the deft accuracy for which God is famed. I felt a clear call to stop saying, 'first let me get my children into school, first let me ...', and to get on with ... well, I'm still figuring that out, but I believe part of the call is to write.

When not writing or studying, I teach maths for a living, and spend most of the rest of the time being creative. I live in a messy house in the middle of England full of noise and glue sticks and mess, which I blame on the children, but really it's me.

More Like This

You can get hold of more resources like this, and a lot of them are free! You can find out about my other books at www.fayrowland.co.uk. There you will find info on upcoming titles and samples of other books for free download.

You can use The Reflectionary – my weekly blog of resources for active worship, based on Bible readings used in many churches. Everything is free, so pop along and help yourself at www.reflectionary.org, You can sign up there to have the posts sent straight to your inbox.

You can also follow The Reflectionary on facebook or twitter. Visit www.facebook.com/Reflectionary.org and 'like', or follow @Reflectionary_ (please note the underscore), for links to free resources.

Ask the Author

If you have any questions, comments or feedback, I'd really love to hear from you. No, really, I would. After all, you, dear reader, are the very reason I write. Without you it would all be ... kind of pointless. And a little bit sad.

So why not drop me a line and let me know how you plan to use a script? Or tell me it's complete drivel and you're going to use it as lining for your hamster's cage.

You can contact me via The Reflectionary's facebook page or send email to fay@fayrowland.co.uk

Image Credits

Actors by Flikr user basykes (CCA 2.0)

Angel with mobile phone by Wikimedia Commons user Centralasian (CCA 3.0)

Bucket by Wikimedia Commons user YVSREDDY (CCA 3.0)

Cheeky Kid by Pixabay user PublicDomainPictures CCA 3.0)

Church by Wikimedia Commons user Dwight Burdette (CCA 3.0)

Happy Puppet by Deviant Arts user lolawolfcandy CCA 3.0)

Indian Drama by Wikimedia Commons user Biswarup Ganguly CCA 3.0)

Shock-ed by Flikr user David Goehring (CCA 2.0) (altered)

All other images © the author or public domain (CCA 0.0)

Angel with mobile phone statue is on the Cathedral of St. John in 's-Hertogenbosch, North Brabant, Netherlands. Sculpted by by Ton Mooy.

Bible Credits

The Message. Copyright © 1993, 1994, 1995, 1996, 2000, 2001, 2002 by Eugene H. Peterson

New International Version - UK

Holy Bible, New International Version® Anglicized, NIV® Copyright © 1979, 1984, 2011 by Biblica, Inc.® Used by permission. All rights reserved worldwide.

Made in the USA
Las Vegas, NV
25 May 2024